I'm sorry But For some Reason Dr. Heyer thought you might Like this... Read the Forword, then Enjoy the Ride Called "Bob". —KKF

Post Cards From Bob

by KK Forss

Published by Beaver's Pond Press
5125 Danen's Drive
Edina, MN 55439-1465
(952) 829-8818
www.beaverspondpress.com

Beaver's Pond Press, Inc.

ISBN: 1-931646-88-0

KKForss@Yahoo.com

Copyright 2003
All Rights Reserved
by KK Forss
and Paul Damon

Printed and bound by
Lightning Printing
Richfield, Minnesota, U.S.A.

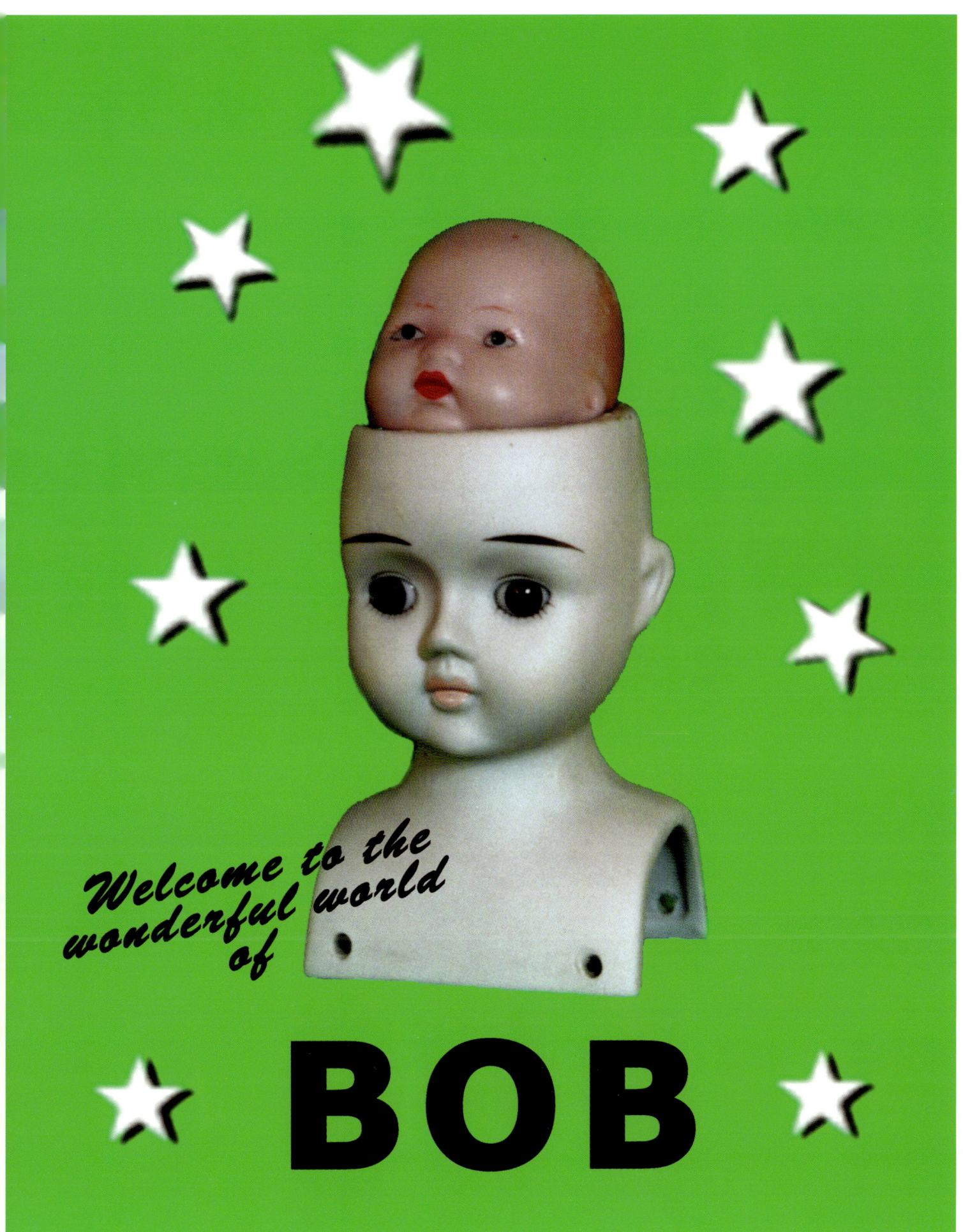

Forward - By Bob

OK, so Here's what ~~this~~ is all About. I Need ~~Cash~~ Campaign Funds. I've Decided to run for Governor in the ~~state of Mines Minnas~~ Minnesota, so the odds are I've got a good shot at winning. To be honest, I guess I have to stay in ~~Minnas~~ the state (At least ~~thats~~ what My parole officer Dude Keeps telling Me) so I figure if I've got to stay here I might as well run the place. That brings us back to the Money... I Need it and so does my Bookie (p.d.) so we put together this book. It's filled with copies of postcards from me to the Love of my life, Susan. Now you can buy the book (A lot of Copies please) and get to Know me better.

One more thing, please send ~~money~~ Campaign Donations (Cash works best).

— Bob

Vote Bob
Vote often
Change your clothes and vote Again

Front

BACK

Dear Susan,
Started putting up campaign posters.
What Does "NO Trespassing" Mean?
— Bob

To Susan
7246 Penn Ave #12
Richfield, MN
55423

Vote Bob
Vote often
Change your clothes and Vote Again!

Front

Back

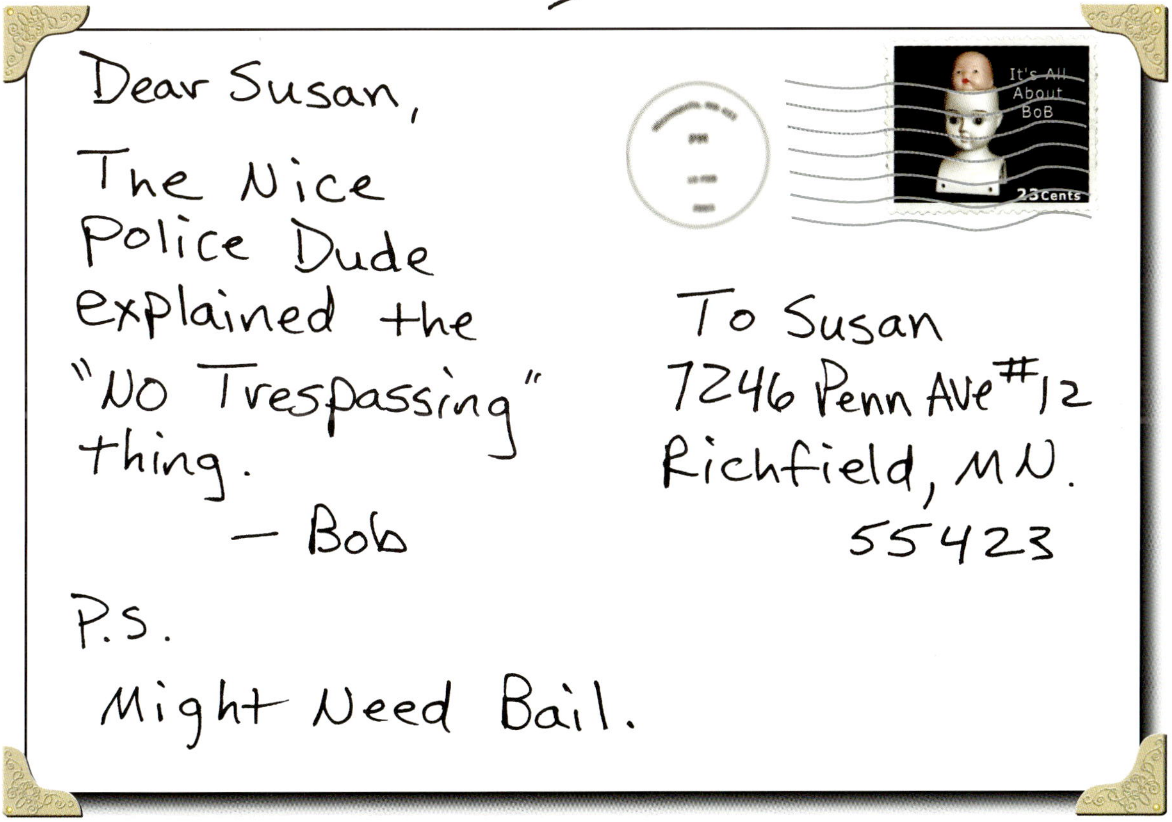

Dear Susan,
The Nice Police Dude explained the "No Trespassing" thing.
— Bob

P.S. Might Need Bail.

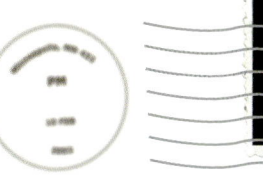

To Susan
7246 Penn Ave #12
Richfield, MN.
55423

Front

Back

Dear Susan,
Made Bail!
Went out to
Celebrate.

    Who's the Man?
    Bob's the Man,
      — Bob

P.S.
Bartender Chick thinks Bob's Hot!

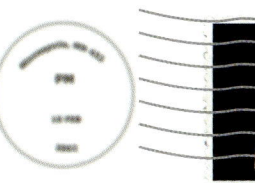

To Susan
7246 Penn Ave #12
Richfield, MN
    55423

Front

Back

Dear Susan,
Had a little too much fun last night.
Not sure who put me here.
 Bobs pretty Pissed,
  — Bob
P.S. Kind of worried, The Little Rabbits looking At Me Funny.

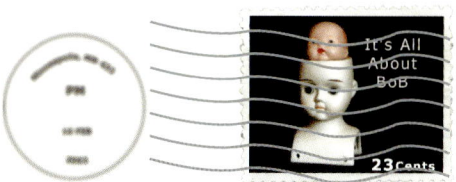
It's All About Bob
23 Cents

To Susan
7246 Penn Ave #12
Richfield, MN
 55423

Front

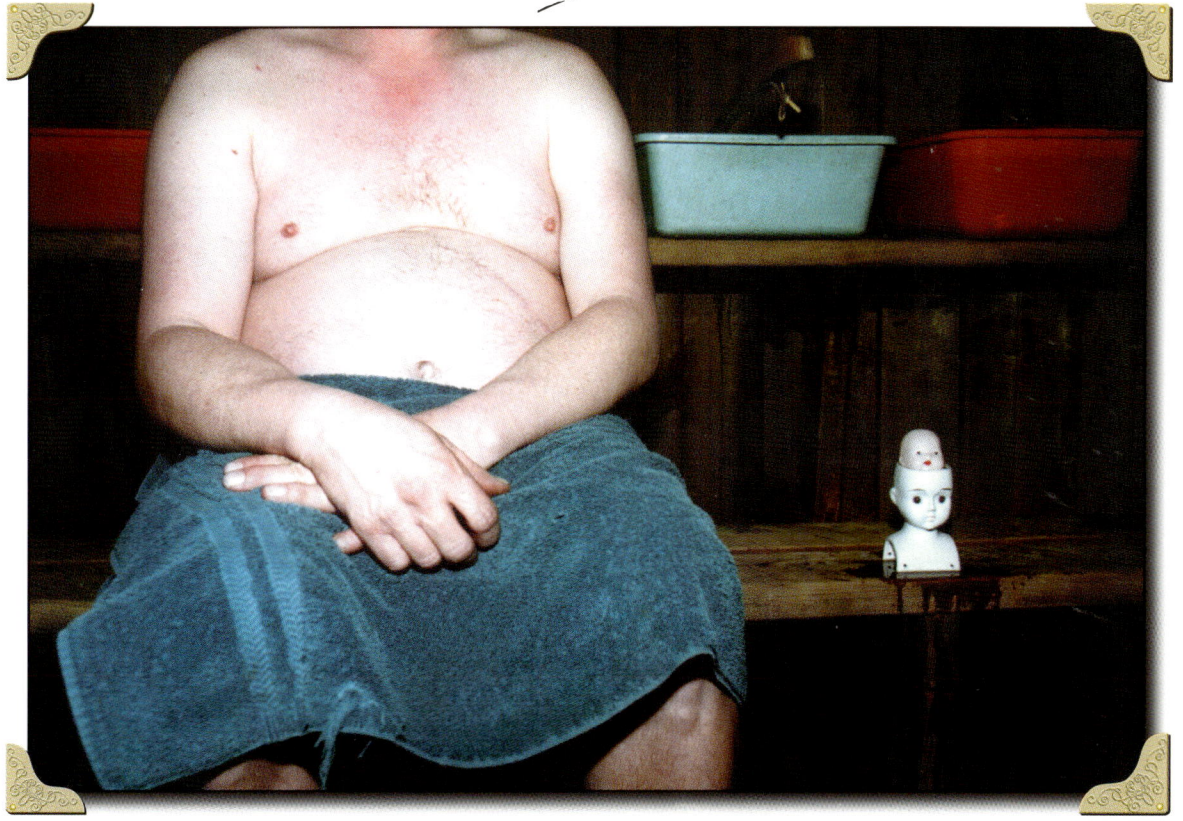

Back

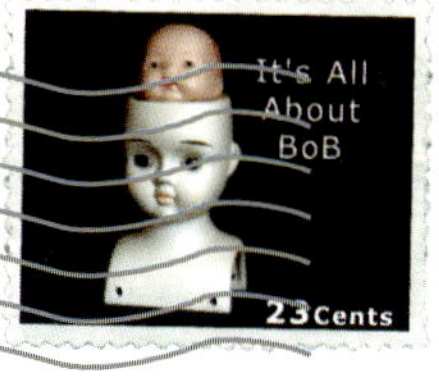

Dear Susan,
Took a Sauna.
Pretty sure I met
the ~~Body~~ Govenor.
Bobs the Man,

— Bob

Vote Bob

To Susan
7246 Penn Ave #12
Richfield, MN.
55423

Front

BACK

Dear Susan,

 Been Having a Little squirrel Problem.

 Hope your well,

 — Bob

To Susan
7246 Penn Ave #12
Richfield, MN.
 55423

Front

Back

Dear Susan,
Gave an interview.
Did Great.
— Bob

P.S. whats A Platform?

vote Bob
vote often
Change your clothes and vote Again

To Susan
7246 Penn Ave #12
Richfield, MN
55423

Page 13

Front

Back

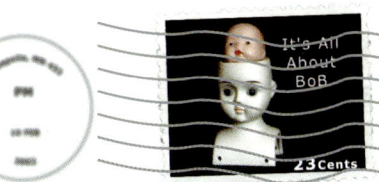

Dear Susan,
Found out that if you give Santa a bunch of money up front, she takes you back to her room and asks you what you want for Christmas.
<u>Santa Rocks!</u> — Bob
P.S. Can you send money?
I want to go see Santa again.

To Susan
7246 Penn Ave #12
Richfield, MN
55423

Front

Back

Dear Susan,
Went to go see Santa Again... Pretty Sure She's Not the Real Santa.
— Bob

P.S. Might Need Bail.

To Susan
7246 Penn Ave #12
Richfield, MN.
55423

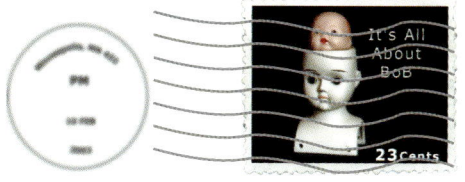

Front

Back

Dear Susan,
Had A talk with the waitress chick. She seems to think that when I send you postcards it might violate that "Restraining order" thing.
   Kind of Confussed,
      — Bob
P.S.
How come you Never write Back?

To Susan
4255 Lyndale Ave.
Mpls   MN
   55409

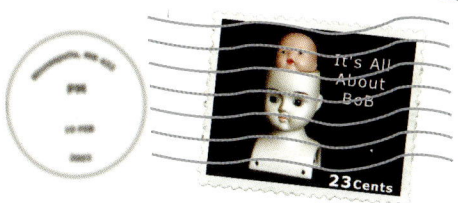

Front

Back

Dear Susan,

Met A Chick!

— Bob

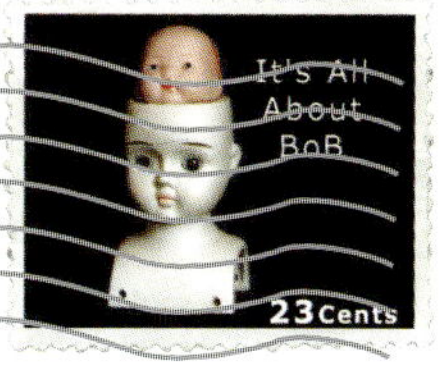

To Susan
4255 Lyndale Ave
Mpls, MN.
  55409

Front

BACK

Dear Susan,
Got a Great deal on some of that Indoor Bathroom Advertising stuff...
Bought a lot of It.
    Bobs the Man,
        — Bob

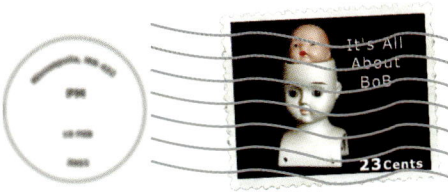

To Susan
4255 Lyndale Ave
Mpls, MN.
    55409

Front

BACK

Dear Susan,
Met a sled dog.
He seems competent.
— Bob

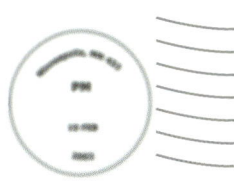 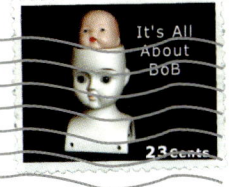

To Susan
4255 Lyndale Ave
Mpls, MN.
55409

Vote Bob

Page 25

Front

Back

Dear Susan,
Great DAY!
Figured out were my Neighbor Hides her spare Key.
She showers at the same time every day.
    Bobs the Man,
        — Bob

To Susan
4255 Lyndale Ave
Mpls MN
       55409

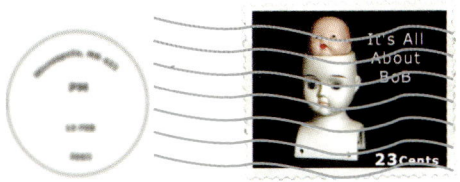

Front

Back

Dear Susan,
Told My Neighbor That I made copies of her spare key.
  Bobs Been Better,
    — Bob

P.S. Forgot to tell her about the Shower thing

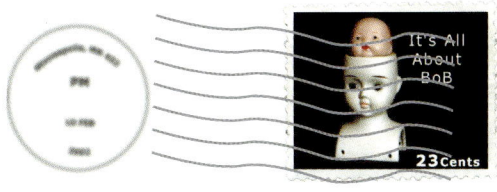

To Susan
4255 Lyndale Ave
Mpls, MN
  55409

Page 29

Front

Back

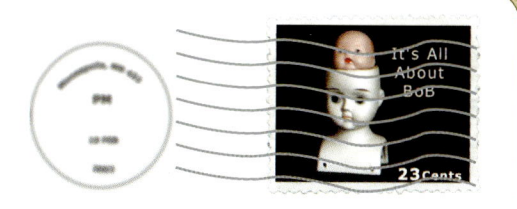

Dear Susan,
 Needed Help putting up campaign posters. Hired An Assistant, He Seems Competent.

   Bob's the Man,

      — Bob

To Susan
4255 Lyndale Ave
Mpls, MN.
     55409

Front

Back

Dear Susan,

Sisters...

Bobs Feeling Lucky,
— Bob

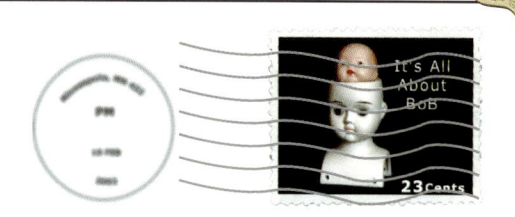

P.S.
whats a Chainsaw?

To Susan
4255 Lyndale Ave
Mpls, MN.
55409

Page 33

Front

Back

Dear Susan,
The Campaign is Capturing the Imagination of the world.

It's All About Bob,
— Bob

Vote Bob
Vote often
Change your clothes and Vote Again

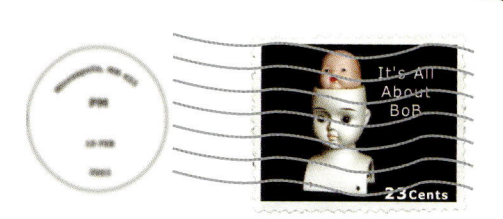

To Susan
4255 Lyndale Ave
Mpls MN
55409

Page 35

Front

Back

Dear Susan,

The New Assistant is Working Out Pretty Good!

Bob's the Man,
— Bob

It's All About BoB
23 Cents

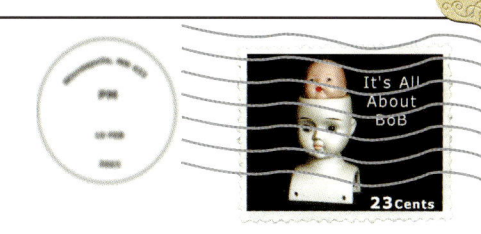

To Susan
4255 Lyndale Ave
Mpls MN
     55409

Page 37

Front

BACK

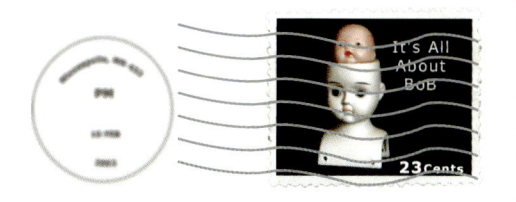

Dear Susan,
went over to
see my
Neighbor.
she showers at
the same time
every day.
who's the Man?
Bob's the Man,
— Bob

To Susan
4255 Lyndale Ave
Mpls MN
55409

It's All About BoB
23 cents

Front

Back

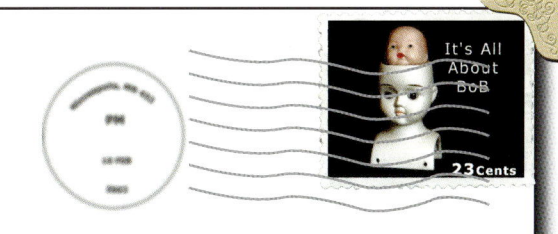

Dear Susan,
My Neighbor
Put the Blinds
Down.

   Bob's pretty
    Bummed,
     — Bob

Vote Bob!

To Susan
4255 Lyndale Ave
Mpls, MN.
     55409

It's All About BoB
23 Cents

Page 41

Front

Back

Dear Susan,
Decided I needed security.
Meet Melvin.
He seems competent.
— Bob

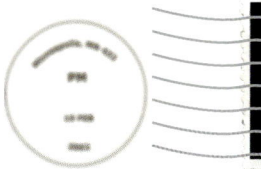

To Susan
4255 Lyndale Ave
Mpls MN
55409

Front

BACK

Dear Susan,

Got a New Hobby...

Might Need Money.
— Bob

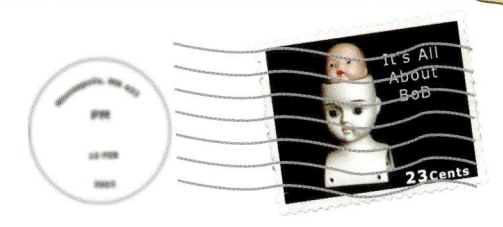

To Susan
4255 Lyndale Ave
Mpls MN 55409

Vote Bob
Vote Often
Change your Clothes and Vote Again

Page 45

Front

Back

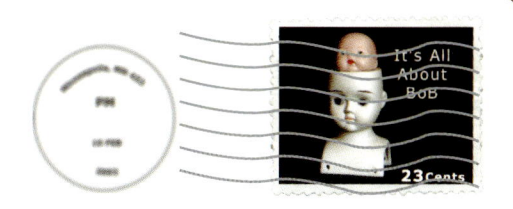

Dear Susan,
Got inducted into the Libertarian Hall of Fame. I Guess I took the place of some Nobels Prize winning Dude.
— Bob

P.S.
I won 5 bucks in slots once.

To Susan
4255 Lyndale Ave
Mpls MN
 55409

Front

Dirty Harry (1971), Any Which Way You Can (1980), In the Line of Fire (1993), "The Bridges of Madison County" (1995), and Absolute Power (1997).

His 1992 Western Unforgiven earned him Oscars for Best Picture and Best Director.

He was mayor of Carmel, California, from 1986-1988.

Quotable

Playboy: "How would you characterize yourself politically?"

Eastwood: "Libertarian... Everyone leaves everyone else alone." -- Playboy Interview, March 1997.

any difference. All th... Libertarians."

About the Libertarian Party, Party is, by far, the very larg... Republicans and Democrats various offices all over the c... Libertarians gain more regi... the two big parties. They a... many people see as) the tir...

Downs' distinguished care... nearly 60 years. In 1985, he Book of World Records as h... greatest number of hours o... television.

Bob - this remarkable warrior for personal freedom rose thru the ranks as a Champion of Humanity.

Bob overcame personal hardships early in life - i.e.: 32 counts of public intoxication and indecent exposure, but refused to let the Man keep him down.

Bob will be remembered for the profound Social Commentary in the famous speech "I am Bob"

John Laroquette

John Laroquette is a 4-ti... to millions of Americans... shows such as "Night C... Show."

Quotable
On Tom Snyder's "Late... guest host Jon Stewart t... member of the Libertari... libertarians are "serious...

Back

Dear Susan,

I keep forgetting to Ask, whats a Libertarian Anyway?

    Bob's the Man,
      — Bob

P.S.
Who's Clint Eastwood?

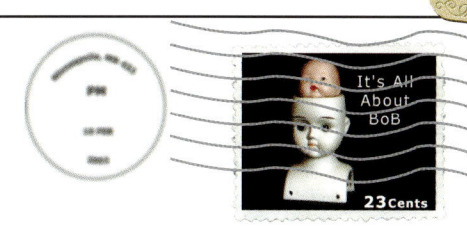

To Susan
4255 Lyndale Ave
Mpls MN
55409

Stamp: "It's All About BoB" 23 Cents

Front

Back

Dear Susan,
Went Bird
Watching...
Having serious
issues with one
of those Birds.
Bob's pretty pissed,
— Bob

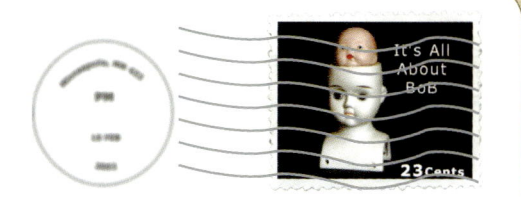

To Susan
4255 Lyndale Ave
Mpls MN
55409

Page 51

Front

Back

Dear Susan,
It was great to hear from you. My heart soared when the nice policeman told me that you sent your regards!
 Love Always,
  — Bob
P.S.
Might Need Bail

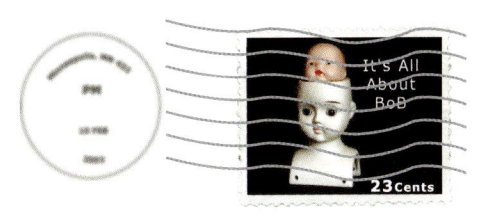

To Susan
4255 Lyndale Ave
Mpls MN
55409

Page 53

Front

Back

Dear Susan,
Learning to swim, Hired an instructor.

He seems competent.
— Bob

Vote Bob

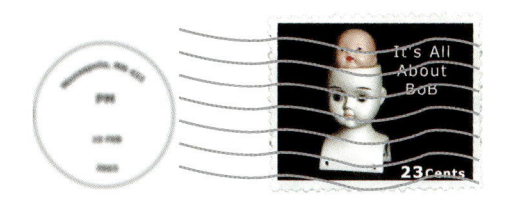

To Susan
9432 Grand Ave #4
Bloomington, MN
55420

It's All About Bob
23 cents

Front

Back

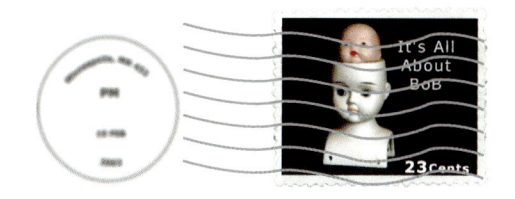

Dear Susan,
Had A strategy meeting At Campaign HeadQuarters. Pretty sure we talked about... something.
Bob Needs ~~Aspirin~~ Morphine Drip.
— Bob

Vote Bob
Blah, Blah, Blah

To Susan
9432 Grand #4
Bloomington, MN
55420

Page 57

Front

Back

Dear Susan,
Bought A
Car.

— Bob

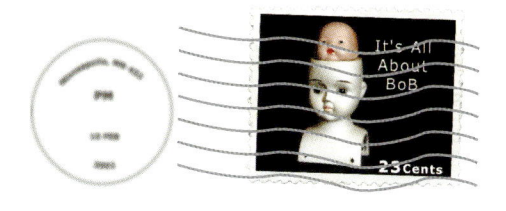

To Susan
9432 Grand Ave #4
Bloomington, MN.
55420

It's All About BoB
23 Cents

Page 59

Front

Back

Dear Susan,
My Bookie came over.
Pretty Sure I owe him Money.
— Bob

Vote Bob
Vote Often
Change your Clothes and Vote Again

To Susan
9432 Grand #4
Bloomington, MN.
55420

Front

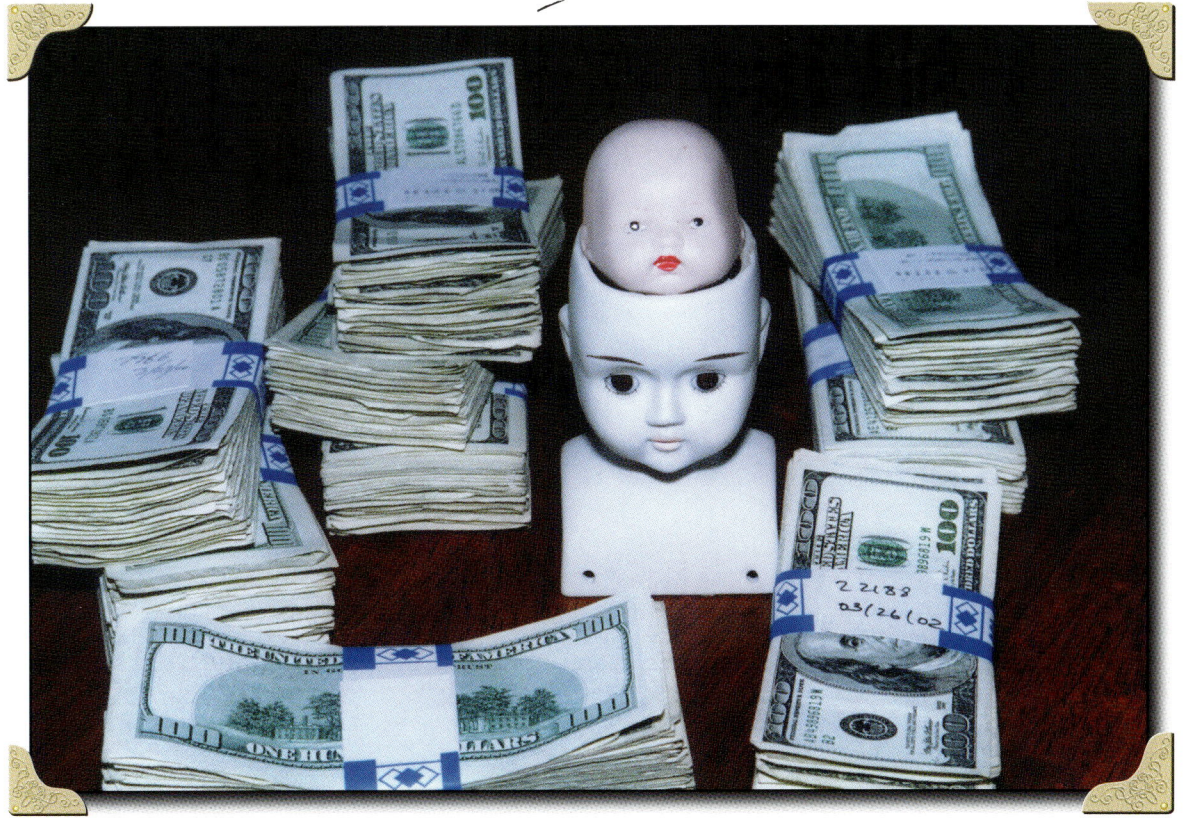

BACK

Dear Susan,
Bob Scores!
Found out people give you money when your running a campaign.
Bob's going shopping,
— Bob

To Susan
9432 Grand #4
Bloomington, MN
55420

It's All About Bob
23 Cents

Page 63

Front

BACK

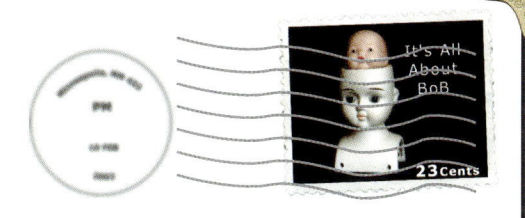

Dear Susan,
Been spending the Campaign Money. Found a Great painting. Pretty Sure it's Gonna be worth Millions.
   Bob knows Art,
      — Bob

To Susan
9432 Grand #4
Bloomington, MN.
      55420

It's All About BoB
23 Cents

Page 65

Front

Back

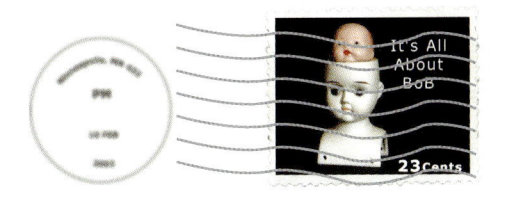

Dear Susan,
My Bookie came over.
Showed Him my New painting!
— Bob

To Susan
9432 Grand #4
Bloomington, MN
55420

P.S. Not sure if He's voting Bob or Not

Front

BACK

Dear Susan,
Hired a Maid. Kind of Bummed though. She actually has clothes that she wears to work. **THAT WAS NOT PART OF THE DEAL.**
   Bob could Be Better,
        — Bob
Got to Go, Looks Like my Bookies Here.

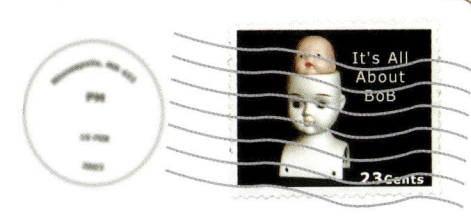

To Susan
9432 Grand #4
Bloomington, MN
55420

Page 69

Front

Back

Dear Susan,
Fired Melvin.
Melvin and Bob were having Personal Space Issues...
Melvin thinks Bob's Hot.
— Bob

P.S. Bob's Pretty Nervous.

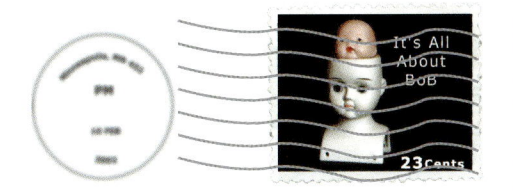

To Susan
9432 Grand #4
Bloomington, MN.
55420

It's All About Bob
23 Cents

Page 71

Front

Back

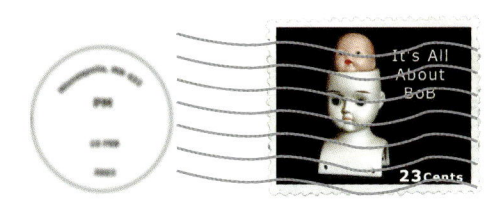

Dear Susan,
Forgot My Key.
Pretty sure I
should have
stayed in the
car.
    Bob's Been Better,
      — Bob

P.S.
Bob's Movin' south

To Susan
9432 Grand # 4
Bloomington, MN.
    55420

Page 73

Front

Back

Dear Susan,
Learning Karate.
Hired an Instructor.
He Seems Competent

Karate's cool

Bob's the Man,
— Bob

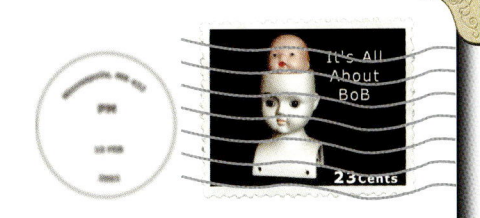

To Susan
9432 Grand #4
Bloomington, M.N.
55420

It's All About BoB
23 cents

Front

BACK

Dear Susan,

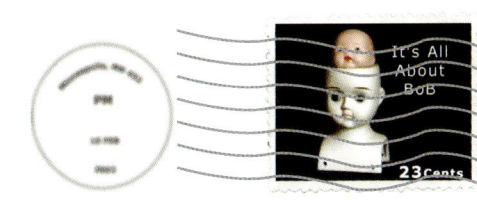

Quit Karate.

— Bob

To Susan
9432 Grand #4
Bloomington, MN.
55420

It's All About Bob
23 cents

Page 77

Front

Back

Dear Susan,
Was Buying ~~Votes~~ Drinks for people. Not sure who put me here.
   Bob's pretty Pissed,
      — Bob

Vote Bob

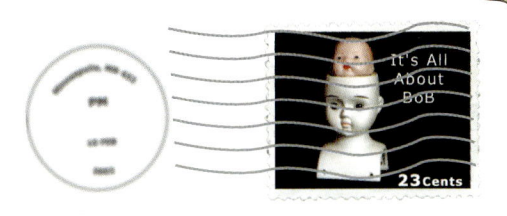

To Susan
5561 Nicollet
Mpls, MN.
   55419

Page 79

Front

Back

Dear Susan,
I've heard of Big mouth Bass Before, But Good Golly, this idiot won't shut up.
— Bob

P.S. Gotta Be an off switch here somewhere

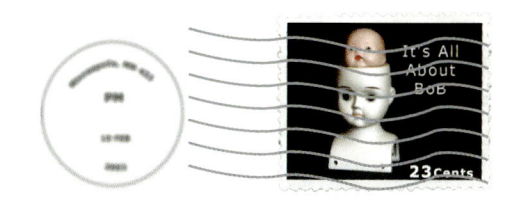

To Susan
5561 Nicollet Ave
Mpls, MN.
55419

Page 81

Front

Back

Dear Susan,

Found an Abandoned House... Gonna Stay Awhile.

— Bob

Got to go, I think the Pizza Dude is Here

To Susan
5561 Nicollet
Mpls, MN
55419

Front

Back

Dear Susan,
I guess the House wasn't Quite Abandoned. How can they call it "Breaking and Entering" if you go in thru the Dog Door?
    Might Need Bail,
        — Bob
P.S. I'm Famous, the Policeman Knew my Name!

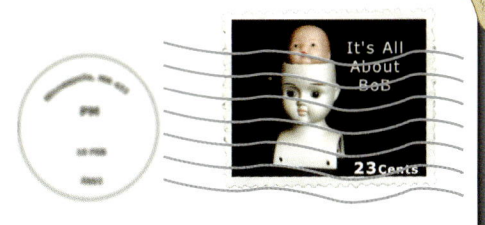

To Susan
5561 Nicollet
Mpls, MN
    55419

It's All About BoB
23 Cents

Front

BACK

Dear Susan,
Found a New Place to Rent. It's Already Furnished in a Great Style... Love the Cabinet Space!
— Bob

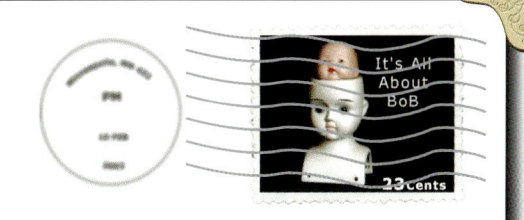

P.S. New Landlord thinks Bob's Hot.

To Susan
5561 Nicollet Ave
Mpls, MN.
55419

Front

BACK

Dear Susan,
Been taking the Campaign Door to Door telling people to "Vote Bob".
— Bob

P.S.
Seen alot of Pretty Shotguns!

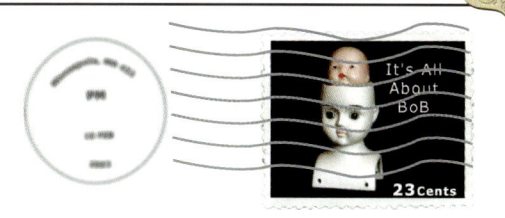

To Susan
5561 Nicollet
Mpls, MN.
55419

It's All About BoB
23 Cents

Page 89

Front

Back

Dear Susan,
Spent the day trying to understand Ice Fishing...
Just Don't Get it,
— Bob

vote Bob

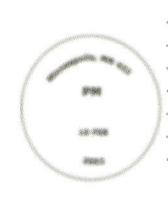

To Susan
5561 Nicollet
Mpls, MN.
55419

It's All About BoB
23 Cents

Page 91

Front

Back

Dear Susan,

Help.

— Bob

Vote Bob
Vote Often
Change your clothes and Vote Again

To Susan
5561 Nicollet Ave
Mpls, MN.
55419

Front

Back

Dear Susan,

Learned How to Breakdance.

Who's the Man
Bob's the Man.
— Bob

To Susan
5561 Nicollet
Mpls, MN
55419

It's All About Bob
23 cents

Front

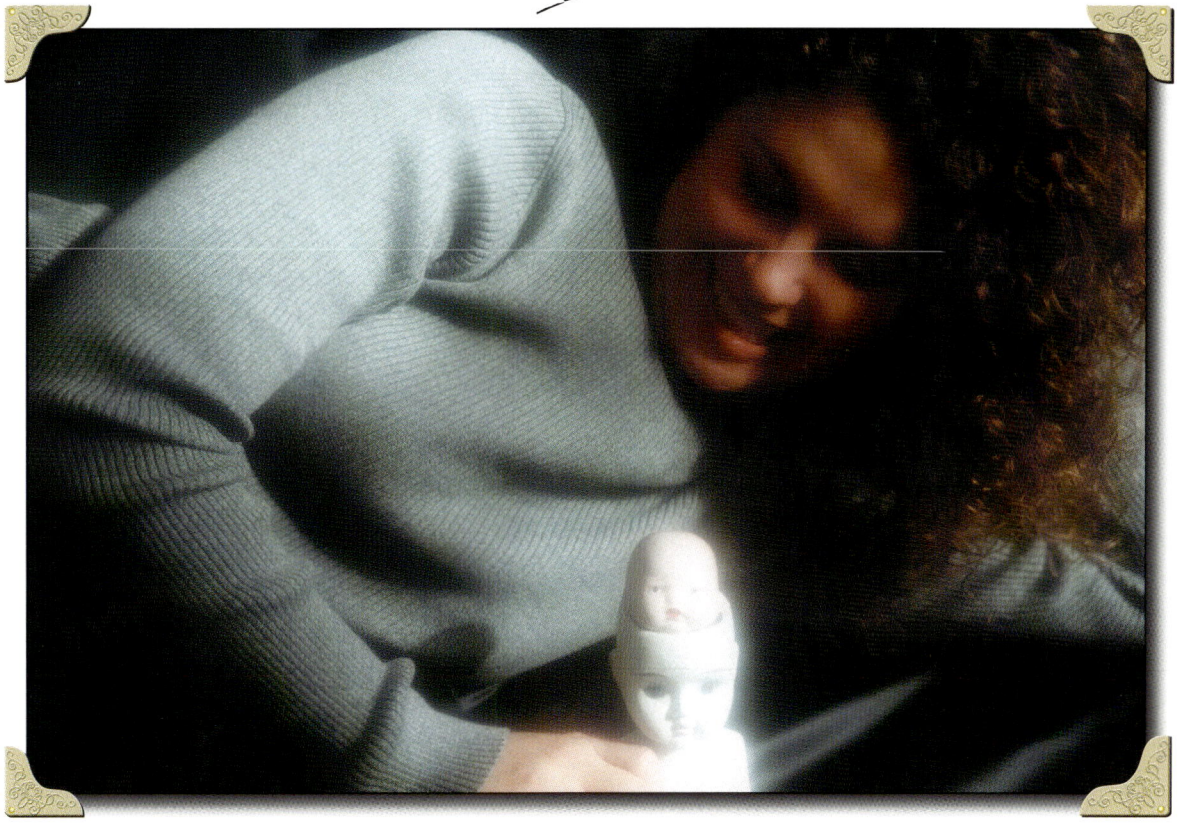

Back

Dear Susan,

Hired a New Assistant... Could care less if she's competent or not.

— Bob

Bob's the Man

To Susan
5561 Nicollet
Mpls, MN.
55419

It's All About Bob
23 Cents

Page 97

Front

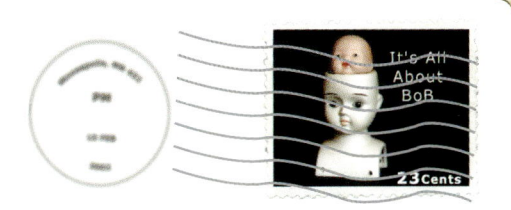

LUKE 2:7

AND SHE BROUGHT FORTH HER FIRSTBORN SON AND WRAPPED HIM IN SWADDLING CLOTHES, AND LAID HIM IN A MANGER.

Back

Dear Susan,
Check it out...
the little kid in the window looks alot like me.
Pretty sure we're related.
— Bob

To Susan
5561 Nicollet
Mpls, MN.
55419

Page 99

Front

Back

Dear Susan,
You should Meet My Mailman, He's really Nice to me. Each time you move and Forget to give me your New Address, I Just Give Him alot of Money and He gets me your New one. You'd Like Him. I'll write Again Soon. — Bob

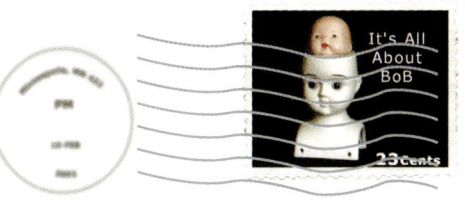

To Susan
5561 Nicollet
Mpls, MN.
55419

Page 101

Front

Back

Dear Susan,
Met your Friend.
He's pretty Cool.
We're going out on his boat so He can teach Me a New Blindfold Game.
 He seems competent
  — Bob
Vote Bob

To Susan
10935 France Ave
Bloomington, MN.
   55431

Page 103

THE END

kind of

Bob out-takes

Page 107

Page 108

Page 109

Page 110

Page 111

Page 112

Page 113

Page 114

Page 115

Page 116

Written and Directed
By
KK Forss

Produced
By
Damon Design
A Paul Damon Company

Computer Graphics
By
Mike Zelenak

The Object of Bob's Affection

Susan McGovern

Cast
in order of Appearance

Bob AS	Bob
Nice policeman	secret
Bartender Chick	Crissy
Rabbits	Daisy, Sophie
The Governor	Kevin
Squirrel	Head Case
Libertarian Dude	Forrest
Santa Hooker	Jeannie
Chick Chick	Katie
Sled Dog	No Idea
Neighbor	Wendy K.
Waitress Chick	Jessica
Assistant #1	Sir Aurther
Cool dude in Mirror	George
Neighbor with Bat	Megan
Melvin	Boomer
Hot Maid	Jeannie
Karate Dude	Kyu
Shot Gun	Dan
Assistant #2	Amanda
Nice Mail Man	secret
Susan's Friend	Mike

People I want to thank (At least some of them)
Mom, Art, Paul, Mike, Susan, Wendy, Wendy, Beth, Pastor Ned, Mark, Brian, The Chick who had the garage sale where I bought Bob, and everyone I'm spacing out on because I have to get this to the publisher this afternoon... Oh yeah, my publisher Beavers Pond Press and Lightning Printing.

Businesses that let me tear their place apart to take pictures.
The Flower Market, Reilly's Pub, VRT, Chicago Costume, Borderland Lodge, Trails End, 58th St. Service, Peters Billiards, Isabellas Fine Lingerie, Wide Angle Records, Dragon Art Glass, Libertarian Party of MN. and Richfield Photo.

Bob Painting Created By Nate Farley

The biggest thanks of all go to God for making me the way I AM, saving me, and loving me even though I'm kind of an odd duck... Gods the Man!